JOURNAL

of

RADICAL
PERMISSION

JOURNAL of RADICAL PERMISSION

A DAILY GUIDE FOR FOLLOWING YOUR SOUL'S CALLING

adrienne maree brown Sonya Renee Taylor

This journal is designed to accompany the Institute for Radical Permission Course that Sonya Renee Taylor and adrienne maree brown are hosting in 2022. You can access the course at radicalpermission.org.

BK

Berrett–Koehler Publishers, Inc.

Dear Radical Human in the Act of Being,

Thank you for the fear-facing choice to open this page and the page after and the page after that. Thank you for giving yourself permission because our individual acts of permission are both a contagion and an antidote. Permission is the cure that, when sipped, unlocks the cells of possibility in others after you. Every loved thing I have ever created in this world has been born of the viral magic of watching some divine being give themselves permission. I'm telling you every contagious thing ain't bad. In 2011, a plus-sized model in a black corset gave herself permission to be juicy and alive in a lingerie ad and it permissioned my sharing of the photo that birthed The Body Is Not an Apology and shifted the trajectory of my life.

You gave me permission today. Just this morning. You didn't even know it, and ain't that how it goes? I woke up in my eighth week of a COVID delta variant lockdown in New Zealand, and the truth is, I felt despairing. As if this black tunnel of isolation might never end.

I was soul lonely today.

Yet I knew you were going to gift yourself permission to pick up this book and begin a liberatory journey into your own divine, incomparable power, and my present self promised your future self that we would meet on this page and begin this journey together. Your permission may have been a dormant seed in you at the time I started penning this letter, and still that dormant seed of permission got me out of bed and showered today. It coaxed me to pray and eat and open a page to write to you. Permission gave your present self and my present self a shared future where we would meet. Permission alters space-time.

Wild, right?

Consider this journal a space to explore the alchemical nature of your own permission. Use it to discover what in you wants to be liberated to its own truth. What small hidden part of you will you allow access to the sun and sky? How can you turn your own base metal into gold?

What I love most about the possibility that lies in these journal pages is that they are certain to illuminate the profound yet overlooked examples of permission you have already unlocked in your life. You have always been your own best cure, and because aboriginal activist Lilla Watson told us ". . . our liberation is bound up together," your cure is contagious. Your permission is an unalterable element in our collective freedom. You, my dear mad, miraculous scientist, hold the key to a thriving future for yourself, your family, your community, the whole of humanity. Yes, you are a key to the whole of humanity, and I pray this journal is a place where you give yourself permission to remember what you already always knew.

Love,
Sonya Renee Taylor

Dearest Liberator of the Self and the Collective,

I want to whisper in your ear: you have permission. You have permission to fully embody yourself, your heart, your gifts, your pain, your brilliance, your love.

My teacher-friend Makani Themba says we are "a millisecond away from freedom." When I hear this, my heart moves in multiple directions. On one path, it's clear that distance is measured by the move from individual to collective—together, we cannot be contained. On another path, I remember the tension of being poised on the precipice of freedom, the freedom to fully become myself, the freedom to understand something new, the freedom to embody something at odds with the shaping of society. And down yet another path is the proximity of freedom, the felt sense of it, the knowing that it is *just* there, *right* there, for all of us, even when it doesn't feel like it.

With this journal, we invite you to leap across time and space to your wholeness, your freedom.

Gloria Anzaldúa said, "I change myself, I change the world." Grace Lee Boggs said, "Transform yourself to transform the world." I read in the Combahee River Collective Statement that "the personal is political." In the waves echoing back and forth between these giants, I understand that there is a work that each of us must do within ourselves that makes more possible for the collective. And I am daunted by the fractal understanding that we will not be able to claim something as a collective that we have not been in the practice of claiming for ourselves, in our bodies, with our time and our decisions, in our communication.

With this journal, we invite you to claim yourself as a territory of change and transformation, an embodied possibility of liberation.

Lorraine Hansberry said, "I am a writer. I am going to write." Chadwick Boseman said, "I am an artist. Artists don't need permission to work." Ayanna Pressley said, "My mother did not raise me to ask for permission to lead."

This is a space where you don't have to ask permission to be you, to be now, to be raw, to be honest, to be free. No one else is going to give you permission to be your wild, unfettered, powerhouse, internal, magical self. No one else can—it will feel like a lie or a push or a chaos or a crisis. When you have permission, you feel free from within, you embody freedom for and with others, and you raise the bar of connection in your life to that of liberatory relationships. This journal is an invitation for you to give yourself permission to live.

Love,
adrienne maree brown

Practices

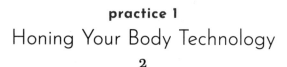

Practice 1

Weeks 1-2: Honing Your Body Technology

"and i said to my body. softly. 'i want to be your friend.' it took a long breath. and replied 'i have been waiting my whole life for this."

—Nayyirah Waheed

Your body is alight with wisdom. Right this minute it is communicating its sacred knowledge to you. Practice 1 is an invitation to tune in to the divine information being conveyed through bone, breath, belly. Over the next two weeks, give yourself permission to be more intimate with your body than perhaps you ever have been, to listen and respond with the fullness of your being. The beginning steps of a life of radical permission requires your willingness to hear and honor your body memories, your sacred and temporary home, and the profound magic therein.

Note: We have provided space for you to journal in response to our questions, but you might need more room! Feel free to use other physical or digital journal space to write until you feel complete. Another option is to answer these prompts outside of this journal so that you can use it over and over.

Assessment and Commitment

....

Let your body answer the question "Why did this journey call to me?"

The next twelve weeks will be a chance to practice more deeply becoming yourself. Create an aspirational statement for yourself, something you can say to remind yourself who you are becoming. (This practice of articulating a statement affirming who you are becoming is inspired by the model of commitment setting from generative somatics.)

DAY 2

Surrender

....

What in my body longs for radical permission?

Surrender

....

Where in my body do I feel my resistance to change? What am I resisting?

DAY 4

Surrender

....

Where in my body can I feel the desire to run, dance, flow?

What am I running from or toward? What is the source of my flow?

DAY 6

Curiosity

....

What old ideas of myself am I ready to release?
Where in my body am I holding these ideas?

Curiosity

....

What do others not see in me that I want seen?

Curiosity

....

What is ripe for change in me? How does my body know this?

Grace

....

What is my relationship to unexpected changes?

Grace

....

What feels graceful in my bones? My muscles?

DAY 10

Grace

....

Where could I offer myself more grace? How can I partner
with my body to do this?

Satisfaction

....

What is one time I remember being satisfied? (It can be a small example or a very large one.) How did my body know?

Satisfaction

....

What would it feel like to let my body be enough, as it is?

Satisfaction

....

What does enough feel like—what does satisfaction
feel like in my body?

DAY 14

Reflection

....

What does it feel like from within when I am in my body?

When I come across a limitation in my body, what wisdom is my body communicating? How can I honor the message (or requests) that my body is communicating?

How can I forgive myself for the times that I have not honored those messages?

What is it I long to experience and feel in this lifetime?

Practice 2

Weeks 3–4: Self-Worship

"I found god in myself and I loved her fiercely."

—Ntozake Shange

You are a manifestation of the divine. This divine is not necessarily a religious divinity, although it can be. It is the realization that whatever energetic force allowed there to be oceans, daisies, streams, buttercups, and oak trees also allowed there to be you. You are no less miraculous than whales and rainbows. What if we chose to be reverent for the divine beauty of the natural world? What if we chose to experience ourselves as a manifestation of that divine beauty and worshipped ourselves as such? Self-worship is your opportunity to locate where you buried your own divine treasure, to excavate it and marvel at its wonder, and to find the rituals and practices that will keep you in divine relationship to yourself.

DAY 1

Assessment

....

What about myself do I already know is worth my worship?

Surrender

....

How have I tried to shrink or hide my divine nature?

Surrender

....

What does it feel like when I surrender to my divine nature?

DAY 4

Surrender

....

How can I surrender to my divinity today?

DAY 5

Curiosity

....

How do I define divinity?

Curiosity

....

What in the natural world calls to me as divine?

DAY 7

Curiosity

....

Where in my own nature do I see similarities to what I see
as divine in the world?

Grace

....

My shadows (the unexplored or seemingly undesirable parts of myself)
are part of my divinity—how do they serve my sacred calling?

Grace

....

How have my shadows protected me?

Grace

....

How can I practice bringing greater love to my shadows?

Satisfaction

....

What actions can I practice that daily remind me of my divine nature?

Satisfaction

....

How do I increase my capacity to be worshipped by myself?

Satisfaction

....

What is satisfying about my time alone?

Reflection

....

Using your answers from the Day 6 and Day 7 prompts, write your own two-sentence declaration of self-worship.

Practice 3

Weeks 5-6: Loving Your Shadows

*"Pain is important: how we evade it, how we succumb to it,
how we deal with it, how we transcend it."*

—Audre Lorde

Our shadows, the most disavowed elements of our identities, are essential elements of our humanity. The highest permission we can grant ourselves is the permission to be fallible, to make mistakes, to be wrong, to be the person who caused the harm. Only then can we be fully accountable and ultimately reconciled to the full breadth and scope of our divinity. Practice 3 will help you honestly and compassionately access and embrace your shadows.

DAY 1

Assessment

....

What shadow parts of myself do I hide?

Surrender

....

Who am I fighting? How am I fighting?

DAY 3

Surrender

....

Where can I soften, becoming more compassionate
with my shadows?

DAY 4

Surrender

....

What would it mean for me to surrender to the fact that I have been harmed and I have caused harm? How can I practice this surrender?

Curiosity

....

Who has withheld permission from me in my life?

Curiosity

....

Who has given me permission in my life?

Curiosity

....

Can I get curious about my own patterns of harm and their root systems?

What will I do to explore these patterns?

Grace

....

How can I maintain my dignity in moments of accountability?

What must I do to understand that accountability is an act of dignity?

DAY 9

Grace

....

How can I bring more love to the parts of me I find unlovable?

DAY 10

Grace

....

In what areas of my life could I be more gracious and graceful?

Satisfaction

....

How can I learn to be satisfied as a being who has both light and shadows?

Satisfaction

....

How can I embrace my shadows as an essential aspect of my life's journey?

DAY 13

Satisfaction

....

What practice can I build around lovingly acknowledging
my imperfections?

Reflection

....

What is my daily affirmation in honor of my shadow self?

Practice 4

Weeks 7-8: Mutual Worship

"Take a lover who looks at you like maybe you are magic."
—from the poem *Frida Kahlo to Marty McConnell*

Lover, friend, family, community. . . you deserve to have your brilliance reflected in the faces and heard from the mouths of those you love. You have permission to care and be cared for, for no other reason than because you are you. In this practice you will explore who you allow to celebrate you. Who do you allow to herald your majesty to you so that you might witness how miraculous you truly are? Who do you openly worship? Who are you openly worshipped by? Where is mutuality in your relationships? The act of mutual worship is your invitation to consider your divine right to reciprocity and care in your relationships. Here you will practice giving yourself permission to be held and supported.

DAY 1

Assessment

....

Where and when have I denied myself the care and support I most desire?

Surrender

....

How can I surrender to the support I actually need?

Surrender

....

How do I surrender to truly being seen and known?

DAY 4

Surrender

....

How can I surrender to the truth of interdependence?

Curiosity

....

What's in the way of my being known and seen and, in turn,
knowing and seeing others? How can I move that obstacle?

DAY 6

Curiosity

....

In what areas of life have I closed myself off to support
and care from others?

DAY 7

Curiosity

....

What external support could I seek that would increase
and deepen my relationships?

Grace

....

What is care to me? How do I currently practice giving and receiving care? How can I bring more care (as I define care) into my relationship connections?

Grace

....

How can I practice vulnerability with those I love?

Grace

....

How can I honor the parts of me and others that fear
being known and seen?

Satisfaction

....

How can I bring my attention to what is satisfying

within each connection?

Satisfaction

....

How can I more courageously name my needs?

Satisfaction

....

How can I more lovingly listen to the needs of others?

Reflection

....

What dynamics are present in my most enriching relationships?
What do I offer? What do others offer to me?

Practice 5

Weeks 9-10: Life Alignment

"Transform yourself to transform the world."

—Grace Lee Boggs

Permission giving, in its most potent form, is about activating the divine purpose of your very existence. You are an indispensable thread in the tapestry of humanity, and your unique purpose is to contribute to the collective possibility of all life, however that may manifest. Practice 5 invites you to give yourself permission to uncover your particular, irreplicable purpose. The questions in this practice will help you open to your divine purpose with power, joy, and a resounding YES to your gifts.

Assessment

....

What do I believe I am here on this planet, at this time, to do,
to be, to create, or to offer to the collective?

Surrender

....

How can I trust my divine assignment?

DAY 3

Surrender

....

How does my divine assignment serve the collective good, the whole?

DAY 4

Surrender

....

What beliefs must I release to more powerfully step into my divine assignment?

DAY 5

Curiosity

....

What are some principles that I want to guide my choices,
my behavior?

DAY 6

Curiosity

....

What are the conditions that allow me to be most aligned
with my principles?

Curiosity

....

Where is there tension between my principles and how I am moving

through life?

Grace

....

Where is grace needed in the way I think of and speak of myself?

DAY 9

Grace

....

Where is grace needed in my relationships?

Grace

....

Where is grace a part of my life's work?

Satisfaction

....

What are the greatest areas of contentment in my life currently?

Satisfaction

....

If I had total permission, what would change in my life?

Satisfaction

....

From where I am today, will I be pleased at the end of my life's journey?
If not, what needs to shift?

Reflection

....

What am I discovering about myself that can better aid me in living in my purpose?

Practice 6

Weeks 11-12: What's Emerging?

"There's nothing new under the sun, but there are new suns."

—Octavia E. Butler

The act of giving yourself permission is an ever-evolving process. Each day a new area of awareness may arise where you are given the opportunity to expand into even greater permission and power than the day before. Practice 6 is an invitation to name these new internal landscapes that have surfaced and will continue to surface over the course of this journey. The following inquiries are here to encourage an ever-expanding awareness and honoring of all your emerging bounty.

DAY 1

Assessment

....

What areas of permission have emerged for me in this process?

DAY 2

Surrender

....

How can I more fully welcome the discoveries about myself
that are arising in me?

DAY 3

Surrender

....

How can I more tenderly hold the discoveries of my growing edges?

Surrender

....

What glorious and uncomfortable awareness can I allow to just be?

Curiosity

....

What is exciting about who I am giving myself permission to be?

Curiosity

....

What is uncomfortable or frightening about who I am giving myself
permission to be?

Curiosity

....

What mysteries am I discovering in myself?

DAY 8

Grace

....

What am I learning about the relationships I need to be in now?

DAY 9

Grace

....

In what areas of my life am I able to operate with grace?

DAY 10

Grace

....

Who else would I like to gift access to the overflow of my grace?

DAY 11

Satisfaction

....

What am I giving myself more permission to do today?
Who am I giving myself permission to be today?

DAY 12

Satisfaction

....

Where in my life have I noticed a shift toward greater peace,
power, pleasure, joy, and ease?

Satisfaction

....

Am I satisfiable? How do I know?

DAY 14

Reflection

....

How can I be satisfied with this day?

Practice 7

Harvest

"They tried to bury us. They didn't know we were seeds."

—Mexican Proverb

You have completed this journaling process and hopefully have experienced a dynamic shift in your own act of permission giving. If the shift feels more subtle, like a tight bud just beginning to open, celebrate. That, too, is a transformative gift. Use this harvest space to reflect on your time in these pages and to honor the work you have done to arrive at this point. It has been a brave work.

Self-Evaluation

....

Am I satisfied with this journey? Why or why not?

Self-Evaluation

....

Am I satisfied with my participation? What can I affirm about
how I showed up?

Self-Evaluation

....

What have I learned about the conditions I need to create
for giving myself permission?

Self-Evaluation

....

What am I ready to share with my friends and family?

Dear Brave Radical Friend,

You did it! WOOT WOOT!

Blow the horns, shoot off the streamers, pour a glass of something fizzy and delightful. You have earned it, my dear. We don't celebrate ourselves enough. I hope this process has invited you to step into that permission.

If you are currently feeling like you didn't "do enough," I invite you to return to the opening of this letter and read it again. Yes, go back to the "WOOT!" Whatever you did, whether you wrote scrolls of sacred text or jotted down small gems of genius, it was your valiant effort to unveil more of yourself to yourself, and what a transformative and sometimes harrowing task that can be. All efforts undertaken to their end are magnanimous efforts and we love you for it.

This journal is neither a beginning nor an ending. It is a continuation of an unfolding toward freedom—yours, ours. What a joy to be bound up in liberation with you, friend. Consider this journaling a sort of rolling out of the red carpet so that you might walk the runway of your own divine badassery. I love the visual of freedom being a red carpet. What can I say? I'm bougie! What I know is that you endeavored toward expansion, and as you stretched the very fabric of possibility through this work, you have opened life a bit wider for us all. That is how it works, this interdependence thing. Ain't it glorious that your expansive permission-giving self keeps multiplying the multiverse of liberatory possibility for everyone?

Don't stop here.

Rest. Absolutely. Take all the yummy naps you need, but wake hungry for more of yourself. Take fourth and fifth heaping helpings from this permission buffet. Frolic naked and unapologetic in all the permission you have given yourself and will continue to give yourself. Be audacious and greedy in your pursuit of personal liberty. It really is contagious, and it is also the cure for much of what ails us all.

Love you radically,
Sonya

Dear and Beloved Student of Life,

What have you learned?

Who are you now?

What does it feel like on the precipice of what you want, what you need?

What does it feel like when the permission comes?

We love you, and we love how you love yourself, because we know it was an act of self-love to move toward this journey, to participate, to reflect, to turn to face yourself.

We are so proud of you for the work you've done here in this journal because we know that whether you merely looked at the questions or wrote books' worth of truth down, you did your best.

Each of us has a place within us that is sacred, what Maya Angelou called the "inviolate" place, the place in us that is before and beyond anything that has happened to us. And all of us have lineages of colonization, socialization, oppression, and control that have made us contort, tucking that place away. It is our hope that the questions you answered in these pages put you in deeper touch with that sacred place within you. We know from our own lives that freedom is directly related to being able to live guided by the sacred directions that are printed on the walls of that divine interior.

When we give ourselves permission to live from our most sacred and eternal impulses, we become a north star to others who have not yet imagined how free and connected they could be. When we do this work together, claiming permission in community, we become a constellation, a brightness of beings.

Like the seed that grew to maturity on these pages, permission is something that grows with your attention and practice. You get to begin again and again, the seed-to-tree cycle grows the forest. Claim permission as many times as you need to, in each area of your life.

Shine on, bright beloved!

Love you celestially,
adrienne

About the Authors

adrienne maree brown is the writer-in-residence at the Emergent Strategy Ideation Institute. She is the author/editor of eight books, including *Emergent Strategy: Shaping Change, Changing Worlds;* the New York Times bestseller *Pleasure Activism: The Politics of Feeling Good;* and the first in her novella trilogy, *Grievers.* adrienne is the co host of three podcasts: *How to Survive the End of the World, Octavia's Parables, and The Emergent Strategy Podcast.* adrienne is committed to growing our collective capacity to love.

Sonya Renee Taylor is a world-renowned activist, best selling author, award-winning artist, transformational thought leader, and the founder of The Body Is Not an Apology, a movement and digital media and education company exploring the intersections of identity, healing, and social justice using the framework of radical self-love. The Body Is Not an Apology's content and message have changed the lives of millions of people around the world, shifting how we live in and relate to our bodies and the bodies of others, shifting from a relationship of shame and injustice to a relationship bound by radical love. She is the author of six books, including the *New York Times* bestseller *The Body Is Not an Apology: The Power of Radical Self Love*, now in its second edition.

Berrett-Koehler Publishers, Inc.
1333 Broadway, Suite 1000
Oakland, CA 94612-1921
Tel: (510) 817-2277
Fax: (510) 817-2278
www.bkconnection.com

ORDERING INFORMATION

Quantity sales. Special discounts are available on quantity purchases by corporations, associations, and others. For details, contact the "Special Sales Department" at the Berrett-Koehler address above.

Individual sales. Berrett-Koehler publications are available through most bookstores.
They can also be ordered directly from Berrett-Koehler: Tel: (800) 929-2929; Fax: (802) 864-7626; www.bkconnection.com.

Orders for college textbook / course adoption use. Please contact Berrett-Koehler:
Tel: (800) 929-2929; Fax: (802) 864-7626.

Distributed to the U.S. trade and internationally by Penguin Random House Publisher Services.

Berrett-Koehler and the BK logo are registered trademarks of Berrett-Koehler Publishers, Inc.

Printed in Canada

Berrett-Koehler books are printed on long-lasting acid-free paper. When it is available, we choose paper that has been manufactured by environmentally responsible processes. These may include using trees grown in sustainable forests, incorporating recycled paper, minimizing chlorine in bleaching, or recycling the energy produced at the paper mill.

Library of Congress Cataloging-in-Publication Data

Names: brown, adrienne maree, author. | Taylor, Sonya Renee, author.
Title: Journal of radical permission : a daily guide for following your soul's calling / adrienne maree brown, Sonya Renee Taylor.
Description: First edition. | Oakland, CA : Berrett-Koehler Publishers, Inc., [2022]
Identifiers: LCCN 2021055809 (print) | LCCN 2021055810 (ebook) | ISBN 9781523002429 (paperback) | ISBN 9781523002436 (pdf) | ISBN 9781523002443 (epub)
Subjects: LCSH: Self-acceptance. | Self-esteem. | Self-actualization (Psychology)
Classification: LCC BF575.S37 B75 2022 (print) | LCC BF575.S37 (ebook) | DDC 158.1—dc23/eng/20220106
LC record available at https://lccn.loc.gov/2021055809
LC ebook record available at https://lccn.loc.gov/2021055810

First Edition

30 29 28 27 26 25 24 23 22

10 9 8 7 6

Cover and interior design, illustration, and composition: Marisa Kwek
Creative Direction: Frances Baca
Copyedit and proofreading: PeopleSpeak

adrienne maree brown's photo courtesy of Masterclass, Ramona Rosales, photographer

Sonya Renee Taylor's photo courtesy of INDIVIDUAL studio, Saami Bloom, creative director, Alexa Treviño, photographer.

Berrett–Koehler
Publishers

Berrett-Koehler is an independent publisher dedicated to an ambitious mission: *Connecting people and ideas to create a world that works for all.*

Our publications span many formats, including print, digital, audio, and video. We also offer online resources, training, and gatherings. And we will continue expanding our products and services to advance our mission.

We believe that the solutions to the world's problems will come from all of us, working at all levels: in our society, in our organizations, and in our own lives. Our publications and resources offer pathways to creating a more just, equitable, and sustainable society. They help people make their organizations more humane, democratic, diverse, and effective (and we don't think there's any contradiction there). And they guide people in creating positive change in their own lives and aligning their personal practices with their aspirations for a better world.

And we strive to practice what we preach through what we call "The BK Way." At the core of this approach is *stewardship,* a deep sense of responsibility to administer the company for the benefit of all of our stakeholder groups, including authors, customers, employees, investors, service providers, sales partners, and the communities and environment around us. Everything we do is built around stewardship and our other core values of *quality, partnership, inclusion,* and *sustainability.*

This is why Berrett-Koehler is the first book publishing company to be both a B Corporation (a rigorous certification) and a benefit corporation (a for-profit legal status), which together require us to adhere to the highest standards for corporate, social, and environmental performance. And it is why we have instituted many pioneering practices (which you can learn about at www.bkconnection.com), including the Berrett-Koehler Constitution, the Bill of Rights and Responsibilities for BK Authors, and our unique Author Days.

We are grateful to our readers, authors, and other friends who are supporting our mission. We ask you to share with us examples of how BK publications and resources are making a difference in your lives, organizations, and communities at www.bkconnection.com/impact.

Dear reader,

Thank you for picking up this book and welcome to the worldwide BK community! You're joining a special group of people who have come together to create positive change in their lives, organizations, and communities.

What's BK all about?

Our mission is to connect people and ideas to create a world that works for all.

Why? Our communities, organizations, and lives get bogged down by old paradigms of self-interest, exclusion, hierarchy, and privilege. But we believe that can change. That's why we seek the leading experts on these challenges—and share their actionable ideas with you.

A welcome gift

To help you get started, we'd like to offer you a **free copy** of one of our bestselling ebooks:

www.bkconnection.com/welcome

When you claim your **free ebook**, you'll also be subscribed to our blog.

Our freshest insights

Access the best new tools and ideas for leaders at all levels on our blog at ideas.bkconnection.com.

Sincerely,

Your friends at Berrett-Koehler